Little Bits of Blue: A Collection of Poems

Copyright © 2023 by Juan Diaz

All rights reserved.

Permission to reproduce or transmit in any form or by any means, electronic or mechanical, including photocopying, photographic and recording audio or video, or by any information storage and retrieval system, must be obtained in writing from the author.

Little Bits of Blue: A Collection of Poems is a registered trademark of Juan Diaz.

First printing September 2023

Library of Congress Cataloging-in-Publication Data

Diaz, Juan
little bits of blue: a collection of poems / by juan diaz

Paperback ISBN: 9798398513578

Published by AR PRESS, an American Real Publishing Company
Roger L. Brooks, Publisher
roger@incubatemedia.us
americanrealpublishing.com

Edited by: Katie Ressa
Interior design by: Eva Myrick, MSCP

Printed in the U.S.A.

Little Bits of Blue

A Collection of Poems

A Diverse Journey Through Love, Heartbreak, Anger, and Inspiration

Juan Diaz

To my nephew Derrick.

Thank you for allowing me a taste of fatherhood.

Contents

Introduction i
The Mess 1
The Summer of 1999 3
Hunger & Thirst 4
An Entire Galaxy 5
Untitled #1 6
Live By Example 7
Untitled #2 8
Attic 9
The Wrestling Fan 10
The End of a Religion 11
The Strength Given 17
Continuous Loop 18
LPW 19
Untitled #3 20
Killing Tiny Tim 21
Untitled #4 26
Reading 27
Poems 28
Untitled #5 29

A Thing That My Mom Taught Me	30
About The Author	31

Introduction

Hello there, dear reader. I would like to ask you a question. What comes to mind when you hear the word poetry? Maybe the mere mention of the word whisks you away like a tornado that carries you back to a time when you were in a tenth grade English class listening to your teacher prattle on endlessly about the poetry of Lord Byron or Walt Whitman, creating an endless vortex of boredom that soured you towards poetry forever. Or maybe you start to think about Shakespearean sonnets as their Elizabethan charm grips you in a vise of confusion, making you have a distaste for poetry for the rest of your days.

Whatever the case may be, I'm here to tell you that you can throw those perceptions of poetry out the window. You see, most of us were taught that poetry needs to be written in a particular fashion and have rhythm and meters, but that's not the case (at least not for me). I find that if a person is too focused in rhyme and meter their poetry becomes too mechanical, almost void of emotion and disengages the reader entirely. Not to mention the overuse of complicated metaphors, which may leave a bad taste in tons of readers' mouths and a distaste for poetry altogether.

Don't get me wrong, rhyme and meter have their beauty and purpose within the construct of poetry, yet it can't be denied that some readers can't see themselves within poetry. So, if readers can't relate to poetry, what's the point of its existence? In other words, poetry should be a tool that is used to communicate to the masses, it is not meant to be some form of highbrow literature that is difficult to comprehend. I can't recount the number of times that I would read specific poems and feel totally lost. The frustration in me was overwhelming to say the least.

Fortunately, all was not lost. Recognizing my budding interest in poetry but not oblivious to my frustration in understanding it, my ninth grade English teacher introduced me to the work of Charles Bukowski, a fellow who was as common as they come. By reading Bukowski's poetry, I was able to relate to him because he wrote his poems in plain English and his metaphors weren't difficult to grasp. Truth be told, I had discovered my muse in Bukowski's words. It was like a fire was lit in my heart that illuminated my soul, exposing all of its wounds and scars.

Suddenly, I was writing like a madman. My soul transformed into ink and poured itself onto each page, giving beauty to my pain. It was then that people began reading my work and seeing themselves within every word, something I didn't expect, but am greatly appreciative of. It is my wish that you, dear reader, see yourself in this collection.

The Mess

She told me we couldn't be together
Because pieces of her lie strewn
Throughout the city.

She confessed that some of her
Could be found folded harshly
In the back pockets of jeans
Owned by men who only came
To her when the stomachs of
Their groins were blue and growling
With the hunger pains of lust.

I didn't care.

When she noticed this,
She began to paint portraits
With the breath of her anger,
Allowing me to view her blowing
Cocaine up her nose as a man
Sat next to her, saliva dripping
From the sides of his mouth.

But alas, she finally stopped speaking,
Allowing the portraits she painted
To fade into the darkness
Enhancing her beauty.

Her soul began to run down her face,

Cleansing the shell that housed it
As she realized that I saw her
As one of God's masterpieces.

The Summer of 1999

Memory is the grave where that
Summer lies garnished with our
Innocence and bathed in our tears.
Its corpse still holds the secrets to
The silencing of my screaming soul.

Oh how it opened its mouth wide to
Receive the nourishment from the
Stars that called us their gods
Because they had yet to witness
A love like ours upon this earth.

So the stars praised us by chanting:
"All hail our sweet gods.
The ones whose hearts silence the
War souls, making the devil cower
In a corner of its hell."

The constellations chanted that all
Summer as they clung onto the black
Cloak of night to observe us walking
Hand and hand, becoming one
In the eyes of their worshippers.

Hunger & Thirst

There I laid in bed costumed
In the third year of the first
Decade of my life.

Still clinging onto the ledge of
Childhood while the jagged
Teeth of life's reality graze
My feet, letting me know
That its hunger was harsh
And brutal.

Despite how afraid I was,
However, I wanted to let my
Heart explore its grounds
In spite of its atmosphere
Being toxic to my innocence.

But I didn't care.
I loosened my grip upon innocence's
Ledge and let myself tumble down
Life's gullet, feeling the dampness
Of its tongue as life savored every
Last bit of my innocence, washing
Me down with the apple juice that
Dribbled from Adam and Eve's chins.

An Entire Galaxy

It's big bang shook the foundation
Of my soul at age eleven,
Awakening a need to
Climb out of my flesh
And consummate my
Love for the printed souls
That house themselves
On rectangular planets.
Each atmosphere shrouded
In their genre, giving me
A thrill to breathe, live,
And partake in those
Worlds.

I become the people
Who inhabit them, watching
As they consume every
Inch of me.

I'm now a totally different person,
One who has become acclimated
To the inhabitants' way
Of life, consuming their food,
Speaking their dialect,
Wearing their clothes, and falling
Deeply in love with each planet's
Inhabitants. In short, let me call
These planets books.

Untitled #1

My soul spills forth
Onto the page
So that I may show
The world what
A free spirit looks like
In an imprisoned body.

Live By Example

"Live by example."
I hate when people tell me that.
Those words spew forth from their mouths
With the power of pseudo-knowledge of book smart
Folks whose minds are a desolate wasteland
When it comes to the realities of life.

Oh how they hate
When a cripple's wounds
Sing their songs of lament.
The lyrics seem to fall on them like acid rain,
Stinging and peeling the flesh off their bones,
Exposing the cripples who they hid from the world.

They hate me for this because I made them
Look at their pain and examine it.
They hate to look at my crippled body
Because they can see themselves.

Untitled #2

The stars cried the night
That a drunk driver opened
The door to Death, grabbing
Her by her ankles and
Dragging her out the door
Never to be seen again.

Attic

I went up to the attic today,
The one that sits atop my neck.
Ah, I love how its old rotted wood
Paneling smells of the desperation
Of youth chasing unrequited love
And trying to grab it by its tail.

Yes, this is where mannequins
Are strewn all over the floor,
The remains of loves that
Were once cherished but
Never cultivated, and the
Only sound that bounces off
Of those walls is a grieving heart.

The Wrestling Fan

I went back to the grave site of 1992.
With a thirsty and hungry shovel,
I dug my way to its corpse
Where I once lay my seven-year-old
Head on a pillow to watch Shawn Michaels
Play sweet chin music on his opponents.

Gorilla Monsoon and Bobby "The Brain"
Heanon bickered back and forth in their
Commentary, making us laugh. Yes,
Wrestling was a sport in which superheroes
Were made, carved from soapstone and
Steroids. That's what they were to me:
The Neo-American Gods.

The End of a Religion

This
Poem
Has
No
Form
Broken
From
Stanza
And
Grammatical
Perfection
For
This
Poem
Has
Discovered
That
It
Is
A
Soul
Fashioned
By
The
Hands
Of
God
It

Is
Because
Of
This
That
It
Has
Roamed
Wild
Upon
The
Earth
And
Found
Her
A
Queen
By
Lust
Stained
Blood
And
Beauty
Of
A
Conquistador
With
The
Faded
Glory
Of
Spain

Yes
She
Was
Fashioned
In
That
Image
With
Her
Ancestor's
Beauty
Lying
Upon
Her
Face
While
The
Tienos'
Soul
Melts
Into
Every
Aspect
Of
Her
Physical
Being
Yes
I
Am
Enchanted
By

This
Beauty
For
Love
Had
Never
Existed
Until
Then
It
Was
The
Dawn
Of
Manhood
For
Me
Oh
Yes
Memory
Loves
To
Perform
On
It's
Stage
For
Me
How
Queen
Nab
Would

Take
Me
From
My
Slumbering
Body
Driving
Me
In
Her
Chariot
Where
I
Became
One
With
My
Queen
But
We
Were
Only
Four
Years
Into
The
First
Decade
Of
Our
Lives
She

Became
Rain
Pounding
Steadily
Upon
Roofs
Destroying
The
Sanctuary
And
The
Images
I
Fashioned
In
Her
Image

The Strength Given

I still carry her essence upon my lips.
No longer are they blushing pilgrims
Foreign to a new land.

No, they belong to a warrior who is armored
With love that carries me throughout the
Day with the knowledge that my scarred
Heart is smiling.

Continuous Loop

When my time comes,
I hope that Death's
Cloak tickles my nose,
Sending me on a continuous loop
To exactly September 8, 1998—
The date when innocence died
And manhood began.

My soul became trapped in the vortex
Of her eyes when she first looked at me
For the first time and my soul tried to climb
Out of my eyes to be one with hers.
Yes, bury me underneath that memory
And make it a continuous loop
Where my soul can be housed forever.

LPW

I met her in the fourth year
Of the twentieth century.
College, freshman year;
Lover of poetry she was.

We talked about the different planets
That we visited and how her soul
Was stained with every word
That scarred the surface
With each language spoken
On every planet, for she worked
In a galaxy where each planet
Was crammed onto a shelf.

Oh how she loved and adored
Working in that galaxy of books.
We talked so much that year
That my soul wanted to be one
With hers, but fear cut off my tongue,
Causing my proclamation of love to die.

Untitled #3

She is in pieces all over my bed.
A canvas of orgasms as
The lyrics to *Tiny Dancer*
Stain the fabric of my
Bedroom's atmosphere.
I am touching the hand
Of God.

Killing Tiny Tim

Ah
Yes
The
Minstrel
Show
That
Was
Ejaculated
By
The
Pen
Of
Charles
Dickens
Fuck
You
Dickens
You
Have
Painted
The
Image
Of
A
Crippled
Boy
Upon
My

Face
At
Birth
Muting
All
Of
My
Potential
To
The
World
I
Graduated
College
Receiving
A
Bachelor's
And
A
Master's
And
People
Tell
Me
That
It's
Brave
And
Daring
Meanwhile
A
Person

Who
Isn't
Disabled
Gets
Less
Praise
Than
Me
Because
It's
The
Normal
Thing
To
Do
I
Hate
That
I
Want
To
Strip
This
Tiny
Tim
Mask
And
Spit
On
The
World
And

Yell
I'm
Human
I
Have
A
Brain
A
Soul
A
Hear
I
Am
Man
Who
Has
Sexually
Desired
To
Be
With
Women
Unfortunately
They
Have
Been
Blinded
By
The
Sheen
Of
Tiny

Tim's
Face
Painted
On
My
Face
So
I
Will
Ask
This
Of
You
Please
Wipe
Tiny
Tim's
Face
Off
Of
Mine
And
See
The
Plains
Of
Humanity

Untitled #4

The year 1995 comes to mind.
My first decade of life was completed.
Tupac and Biggie's beef has penetrated
My bedroom walls, giving them
A heartbeat and a pulse.
This is the soul of my child.
I hold it against my heart as it sings to me.

Reading

Reading a book is like a brief
And wondrous love affair.
In the beginning, you find it
Intense and exciting. So much so,
You can't keep your hands off of it.

You want to be in its world 24/7,
Drinking up all of its passion.
However, it ends, you are sad,
But you will always remember
The beauty that it once taught you.

Poems

What are poems but brief moments
Paused and painted with metaphors
And then in the mouths of artists
Infecting their souls with beauty
And knowledge to explore from their beings?

Untitled #5

I do this poetry shit
To show crippled children
What a free spirit looks like
In an imprisoned body.

A Thing That My Mom Taught Me

Because she saw my scars were consuming my soul,
Mom took me into her arms and said,
"Baby, whatever pain is festering in your heart
Do not feed it. Let its hungry pains bloom art
From its belly, becoming a diamond
That will inspire the world."

About The Author

Juan Diaz received a Bachelor's of Psychology from Wilmington University. After four years of study, Diaz decided to write a crime fiction novel titled *Westside Wilmington Chronicles,* which is currently available via Amazon. Diaz currently resides in New Castle, Delaware where he writes poetry and crime fiction.

Made in the USA
Columbia, SC
03 December 2023

27703033R00024